HR-APPROVED WAYS
TO TELL COWORKERS
THEY'RE STUPID

CLEVER ALTERNATIVES FOR THE THINGS YOU'D LOVE TO SAY AT WORK BUT PROBABLY SHOULDN'T.

THIS BOOK IS PURELY FOR ENTERTAINMENT. NO HR PROFESSIONALS CONTRIBUTED TO ITS CREATION

Saying That Will Get You Fired :

"I can't believe you actually pay me for this."

Maybe Try Say This :

"I appreciate the opportunity to contribute to the team!"

Saying That Will Get You Fired :

"This meeting could have been an email."

Maybe Try Say This :

"I think this meeting is a great chance to brainstorm together!"

Saying That Will Get You Fired :

"I'll just do it my way."

Maybe Try Say This :

"Let's collaborate to find the best approach!"

Saying That Will Get You Fired :

"That's not my job."

Maybe Try Say This :

"I'm happy to help where I can!"

Saying That Will Get You Fired :

> "I'm just here for the paycheck."

Maybe Try Say This :

> "I'm excited to make a difference here!"

Saying That Will Get You Fired :

> "I don't see why this is important."

Maybe Try Say This :

> "Could you help me understand the significance of this project?"

Saying That Will Get You Fired :

"I'll do it later."

Maybe Try Say This :

"I'll prioritize this and get back to you shortly!"

Saying That Will Get You Fired :

"I'm too busy for this nonsense."

Maybe Try Say This :

"I have a lot on my plate, but let's tackle this together!"

Saying That Will Get You Fired :

"I don't need to follow the rules."

Maybe Try Say This :

"I'm always looking for ways to innovate within the guidelines!"

Saying That Will Get You Fired :

"I can't stand this place."

Maybe Try Say This :

"I have some suggestions on how we can improve our work environment!"

Saying That Will Get You Fired :

> "I'm too busy for meetings."

Maybe Try Say This :

> "I'd appreciate a more efficient way to share updates!"

Saying That Will Get You Fired :

"No way, not happening."

Maybe Try Say This :

"I'm not sure that will be possible at this time!"

Saying That Will Get You Fired :

"You're driving me insane."

Maybe Try Say This :

"I appreciate your passion, but let's take a step back!"

Saying That Will Get You Fired :

> "Are you serious right now?"

Maybe Try Say This :

> "Could you clarify that for me, please?"

Saying That Will Get You Fired :

> "This is ridiculous."

Maybe Try Say This :

> "I think we're dealing with some challenges here."

Saying That Will Get You Fired :

> "I'm not doing this."

Maybe Try Say This :

> "I'll need to delegate this to someone else."

Saying That Will Get You Fired :

> "No, just… no."

Maybe Try Say This :

> "I'm afraid I'll have to decline this request."

Saying That Will Get You Fired :

"This is so frustrating."

Maybe Try Say This :

"I think we're encountering some roadblocks here."

Saying That Will Get You Fired :

> "I suppose you might be wrong."

Maybe Try Say This :

> "I see where you're coming from, but I have a different perspective."

Saying That Will Get You Fired :

"That's a terrible idea."

Maybe Try Say This :

"I think we should explore alternative solutions."

Saying That Will Get You Fired :

"I'm over this."

Maybe Try Say This :

"I think it's time to move on to the next task."

Saying That Will Get You Fired :

> "You're wasting everyone's time."

Maybe Try Say This :

> "Let's try to be more mindful of our time."

Saying That Will Get You Fired :

"I quit."

Maybe Try Say This :

"I think we need to assess my current workload."

Saying That Will Get You Fired :

"You've got to be kidding me."

Maybe Try Say This :

"That's an interesting perspective."

Saying That Will Get You Fired :

"I don't have time for your drama."

Maybe Try Say This :

"Let's keep the conversation focused on the task at hand."

Saying That Will Get You Fired :

"Please stop talking."

Maybe Try Say This :

"Could we summarize this discussion?"

Saying That Will Get You Fired :

> "I don't care what you think."

Maybe Try Say This :

> "Thanks for your input; I'll consider that."

Saying That Will Get You Fired :

"Why are we still talking about this?"

Maybe Try Say This :

"Let's move forward with the next steps."

Saying That Will Get You Fired :

"This is so stupid."

Maybe Try Say This :

"I see some potential concerns with this approach."

Saying That Will Get You Fired :

"I don't care what the policy says."

Maybe Try Say This :

"I'd love to discuss how we can adapt policies for better outcomes!"

Saying That Will Get You Fired :

> "I don't do coffee runs."

Maybe Try Say This :

> "I'd be happy to help with any tasks to support the team!"

Saying That Will Get You Fired :

"My dog ate my report."

Maybe Try Say This :

"I encountered some unexpected personal challenges."

Saying That Will Get You Fired :

"I didn't think anyone would notice."

Maybe Try Say This :

"I'll ensure better communication moving forward."

Saying That Will Get You Fired :

"I was just trying to have fun!"

Maybe Try Say This :

"I'm committed to fostering a positive work environment."

Saying That Will Get You Fired :

"I thought everyone was on board."

Maybe Try Say This :

"I'll clarify expectations with the team."

Saying That Will Get You Fired :

"Can't we just ignore the problem?"

Maybe Try Say This :

"Let's address this issue proactively."

Saying That Will Get You Fired :

> "I forgot to submit my timesheet."

Maybe Try Say This :

> "I'll set a reminder to ensure it's submitted on time."

Saying That Will Get You Fired :

> "I didn't think it was that important."

Maybe Try Say This :

> "I now see how critical this is, and I'll prioritize it."

Saying That Will Get You Fired :

> "I'll do it tomorrow."

Maybe Try Say This :

> "I'll tackle this first thing in the morning."

Saying That Will Get You Fired :

"I didn't mean to offend anyone."

Maybe Try Say This :

"I appreciate the feedback and will be more mindful."

Saying That Will Get You Fired :

"I don't care about the team's goals."

Maybe Try Say This :

"I'm eager to align my work with our team objectives."

Saying That Will Get You Fired :

"I was just joking!"

Maybe Try Say This :

"Let's focus on constructive feedback instead."

Saying That Will Get You Fired :

> "I'll just wing it!"

Maybe Try Say This :

> "I'll prepare thoroughly to ensure success."

Saying That Will Get You Fired :

"I thought we were allowed to take long breaks."

Maybe Try Say This :

"I'll be sure to adhere to break policies in the future."

Saying That Will Get You Fired :

"I didn't read the email."

Maybe Try Say This :

"I'll make sure to review all communications moving forward."

Saying That Will Get You Fired :

> "I'm pretty sure I know better."

Maybe Try Say This :

> "I'd love to hear everyone's perspective on this."

Saying That Will Get You Fired :

> "That's not my problem."

Maybe Try Say This :

> "I'd like to help find a solution."

Saying That Will Get You Fired :

"I'm not a team player."

Maybe Try Say This :

"I'm working on my collaboration skills."

Saying That Will Get You Fired :

> "I lost track of time."

Maybe Try Say This :

> "I'll manage my time more effectively."

Saying That Will Get You Fired :

> "I thought we were past that."

Maybe Try Say This :

> "Let's revisit this topic for clarity."

Saying That Will Get You Fired :

> "I can't believe I have to explain this."

Maybe Try Say This :

> "Let me clarify to ensure we're all on the same page."

Saying That Will Get You Fired :

"This is boring."

Maybe Try Say This :

"I'd love to explore more engaging options."

Saying That Will Get You Fired :

> "I thought it was just a suggestion."

Maybe Try Say This :

> "I'll take all recommendations seriously."

Saying That Will Get You Fired :

"I don't need help."

Maybe Try Say This :

"I appreciate the support from the team."

Saying That Will Get You Fired :

"I thought I was being funny."

Maybe Try Say This :

"I'll be mindful of humor in the workplace."

Saying That Will Get You Fired :

"I didn't think you'd mind."

Maybe Try Say This :

"I'll check in to ensure everyone is comfortable."

Saying That Will Get You Fired :

"This isn't my fault."

Maybe Try Say This :

"I'll take responsibility and work on a solution."

Saying That Will Get You Fired :

"I'm too stressed to care."

Maybe Try Say This :

"I'd like to discuss ways to manage stress effectively."

Saying That Will Get You Fired :

"I thought you'd appreciate my honesty."

Maybe Try Say This :

"I'll be tactful in providing feedback."

Saying That Will Get You Fired :

> "I don't care what the client thinks."

Maybe Try Say This :

> "I value client feedback and will act on it."

Saying That Will Get You Fired :

"I'm not really a people person."

Maybe Try Say This :

"I'm working on my interpersonal skills."

Saying That Will Get You Fired :

"I'm just waiting for someone else to fix it."

Maybe Try Say This :

"I'll take the initiative to resolve this."

Saying That Will Get You Fired :

"I thought we were friends!"

Maybe Try Say This :

"I appreciate maintaining professionalism in our relationship."

Saying That Will Get You Fired :

> "I thought it was just a formality."

Maybe Try Say This :

> "I'll treat all processes with the attention they deserve."

Saying That Will Get You Fired :

"I'm not going to change my mind."

Maybe Try Say This :

"I'm open to discussing different viewpoints."

Saying That Will Get You Fired :

"I'm busy with my personal life."

Maybe Try Say This :

"I'll balance my responsibilities more effectively."

Saying That Will Get You Fired :

"I thought we were allowed to be late."

Maybe Try Say This :

"I'll ensure punctuality in the future."

Saying That Will Get You Fired :

> "I don't really like meetings."

Maybe Try Say This :

> "I'm open to making meetings more productive."

Saying That Will Get You Fired :

> "I didn't realize my work was important."

Maybe Try Say This :

> "I appreciate the significance of my contributions."

Saying That Will Get You Fired :

> "I'm not a morning person."

Maybe Try Say This :

> "I'll work on adjusting my schedule for better productivity."

Saying That Will Get You Fired :

"I'm just here for the snacks."

Maybe Try Say This :

"I'm here to contribute meaningfully to the team."

Saying That Will Get You Fired :

> "I didn't realize I was interrupting."

Maybe Try Say This :

> "I'll wait for my turn to contribute."

Saying That Will Get You Fired :

> "I thought we were supposed to be innovative."

Maybe Try Say This :

> "I'll align my creativity with team goals."

Saying That Will Get You Fired :

"I'm not good with numbers."

Maybe Try Say This :

"I'll seek help to improve my skills."

Saying That Will Get You Fired :

> "I thought I could skip the training."

Maybe Try Say This :

> """I'll complete all required training."

Saying That Will Get You Fired :

> "I didn't think anyone would notice my absence."

Maybe Try Say This :

> """I'll communicate my availability clearly."

Saying That Will Get You Fired :

"You need to chill out."

Maybe Try Say This :

""Let's take a moment to regroup."

Saying That Will Get You Fired :

> "I don't want to work with you."

Maybe Try Say This :

> ""Let's find the best fit for this project."

www.ingramcontent.com/pod-product-compliance
Lightning Source LLC
Chambersburg PA
CBHW070357230526
45471CB00006B/2608